**Reading
Gems**

# SPACE
# Supper

It was a lazy day during the summer holidays and Pete was bored.

"I wish something would happen!" he sighed.

Suddenly, there was a shower of sparks and a spaceship landed on the grass.

# This book belongs to

..............................................................

Quarto is the authority on a wide range of topics.

Quarto educates, entertains and enriches the lives of our readers—enthusiasts and lovers of hands-on living.

www.quartoknows.com

© 2018 Quarto Publishing plc

First published in 2018 by QED Publishing,
an imprint of The Quarto Group.
The Old Brewery, 6 Blundell Street,
London N7 9BH, United Kingdom.
T (0)20 7700 6700 F (0)20 7700 8066
www.QuartoKnows.com

A catalogue record for this book is ava from the British Library.

ISBN 978-1-91241-381-2

Based on the original story by Caroline tle

Author of adapted text: Katie Woolley
Series Editor: Joyce Bentley
Series Designer: Sarah Peden

Manufactured in Dongguan, China T 18

9 8 7 6 5 4 3 2 1

FSC
www.fsc.org

MIX
Paper from responsible sources
FSC® C104723

A little green alien climbed down a little ladder and skipped over to Pete.

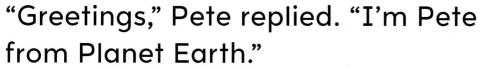

"Greetings," said the alien. "I'm Zub from Planet Flub."

"Greetings," Pete replied. "I'm Pete from Planet Earth."

Zub said that his spaceship had broken down. He would be in trouble with his mum if he was late home for supper.

Zub asked Pete to help fix his spaceship. He showed Pete all the controls. Pete saw the problem. The 'down' button was stuck. Zub would never be able to get back up into space if he couldn't move it.

Pete wiggled it.

Pete jiggled it.

Then he pulled it and he pushed it.

And then...

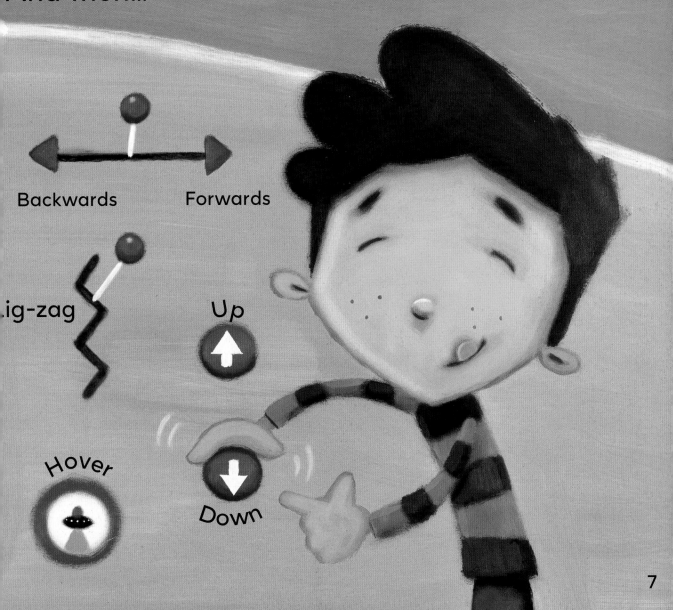

Backwards        Forwards

ig-zag

Up

Hover

Down

Blast off! The spaceship shot up
into the air and zoomed into space.
Zub was on his way home.
But Pete's home was
getting further and
further away.

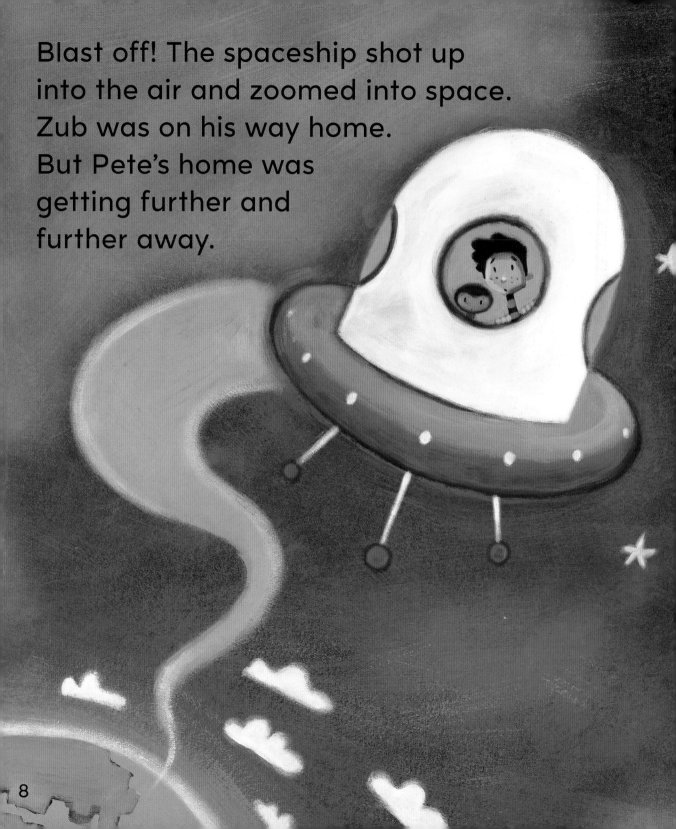

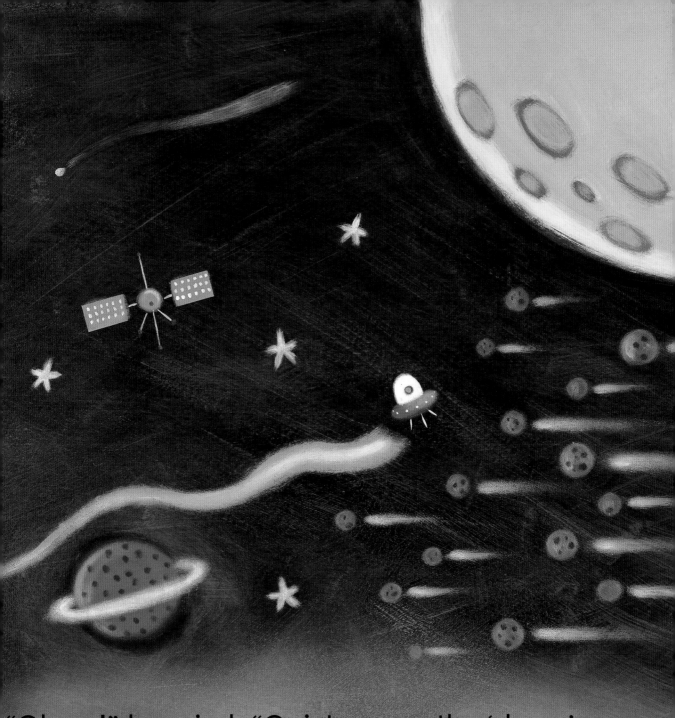

"Oh no!" he cried. "Quick, press the 'down' button again."

This just made the spaceship zoom up higher and higher. There was nothing Zub could do.

"Sorry, it's on autopilot," he smiled. "We'll soon be home on Planet Flub. Mum will know what to do."

"I'm going to be in big trouble if I'm late for supper when I get back," groaned Pete.

Still, there was nothing Pete could do.
He might as well enjoy his space adventure.

The spaceship landed back on Zub's home planet. Zub skipped outside. He couldn't wait to show Pete around.

Zub's mum was waiting for him.

"Zub, you're late," she scolded. "And who is this pink creature?"

"Hello, I'm Pete," said Pete. "I'm from Planet Earth."

Pete didn't want Zub to be in any trouble. He smiled as sweetly as he could at Zub's mum.

Zub told his mum all about his Earth adventure and how Pete had helped him repair his spaceship.

A lot of other green creatures came out to look at Pete. He looked like a funny pink alien.

Zub's mum invited him inside. Everyone sat down at the table to eat some supper.

Pete had no idea what aliens ate but he thought it would be rude to say "no", so he sat down.

They ate zoggle fingers and wiffly wops on wobbly plates. They munched on spiky pies, all washed down with goggle juice. It was delicious!

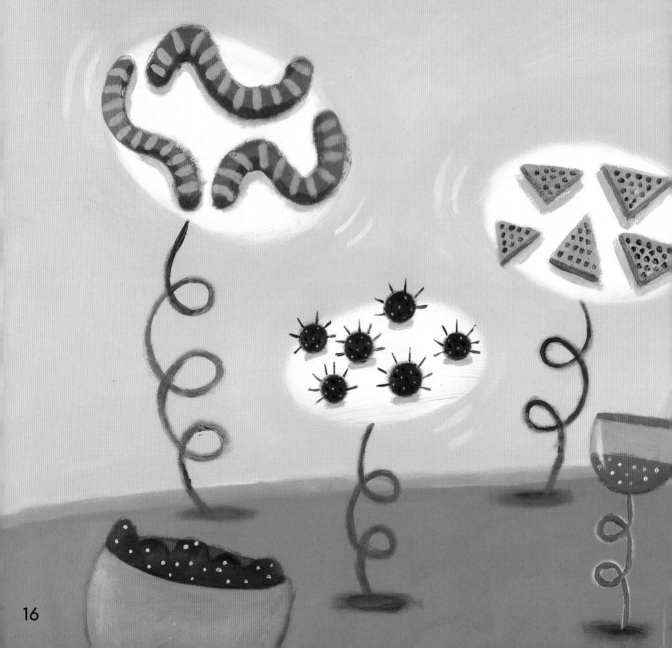

Pete didn't want to go home – he was having too much fun! But his mum really would be cross if he was late.

Pete said goodbye to his new friend.
Zub's mum was going to fly him
home in her Super-Zoom Zippership.

As quick as a flash,
the Zippership zipped and
zapped across the sky.

Pete was beginning to feel
a little space sick!

At last, Pete could see the
outline of Planet Earth outside
the spaceship's window.

Pete raced inside his house and into the kitchen. His mum was just putting the food on the table. It was a fish finger sandwich and a glass of orange juice.

"Hello, Pete," said Mum. "You must be hungry after a day playing in the garden."

Pete wasn't the least bit hungry but he ate it all!

Pete knew his mum would never believe him if he said he'd already had his supper... in space!

Pete couldn't wait until the next day when he was going back to Planet Flub.

Now, the summer holidays didn't seem
o boring after all.

# Story Words

alien

button

controls

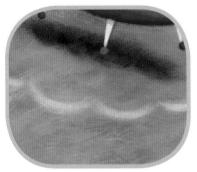

grass

ladder

Mum

Pete

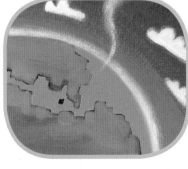

Planet Earth

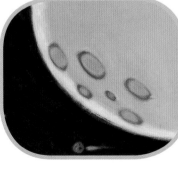

Planet Flub

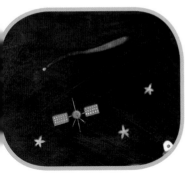

space

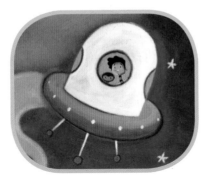

spaceship

sparks

supper

Zub

Zub's mum

25

# Let's Talk About Space Supper

## Look carefully at the book cover.

Which character is on the cover?

Pete is a human boy and Zub is a alien boy. How do they look different?

## The story takes place on two different planets.

Earth is a planet. It is part of our solar system.

Do you know the names of any other planets in our solar system?

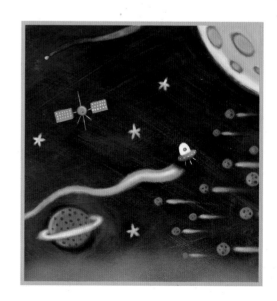

**Pete and Zub eat different food at home.**

Can you think of different meals you eat at home?

What is your favourite food?

What food do you not like?

**Pete is on school holidays and he is bored.**

What activities do you like to do during the holidays?

**Did you like the ending of the story?**

What do you think happened next?

# Fun and Games

Look at the picture of Planet Flub.
Can you find these shapes in the picture?

star      triangle      circle

# Say these words aloud. Does the underlined letter pattern in each word pair sound the same or different?

**a**   Z<u>u</u>b  Fl<u>u</u>b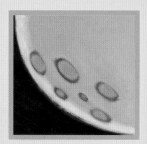

**b**   z<u>o</u>ggle fingers  g<u>o</u>ggle juice

**c**   p<u>ie</u>  fl<u>y</u>

**d**   al<u>ie</u>n  spacesh<u>i</u>p

# Your Turn

Now that you have read the story,
have a go at telling it in your own words.
Use the pictures below to help you.

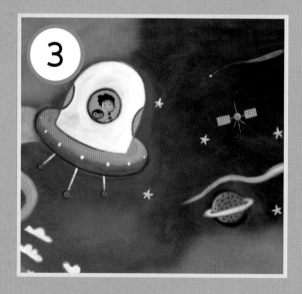

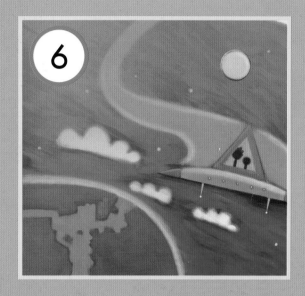

# GET TO KNOW READING GEMS

**Reading Gems** is a series of books that has been written for children who are learning to read. The books have been created in consultation with a literacy specialist.

The books fit into four levels, with each level getting more challenging as a child's confidence and reading ability grows. The simple text and fun illustrations provide gradual, structured practice of reading. Most importantly, these books are good stories that are fun to read!

**Level 1** is for children who are taking their first steps into reading. Story themes and subjects are familiar to young children, and there is lots of repetition to build reading confidence.

**Level 2** is for children who have taken their first reading steps and are becoming readers. Story themes are still familiar but sentences are a bit longer, as children begin to tackle more challenging vocabulary.

**Level 3** is for children who are developing as readers. Stories and subjects are varied, and more descriptive words are introduced.

**Level 4** is for readers who are rapidly growing in reading confidence and independence. There is less repetition on the page, broader themes are explored and plot lines straddle multiple pages.

*Space Supper* follows a boy's journey into space and back. It explores themes of friendship and space adventure.

# Level 4

It was a lazy day during the summer holidays and Pete was bored.

"I wish something would happen!" he sighed.

Suddenly, there was a shower of sparks and a spaceship landed on the grass.

A little green alien climbed down a little ladder and skipped over to Pete.

"Greetings," said the alien. "I'm Zub from Planet Flub."

"Greetings," Pete replied. "I'm Pete from Planet Earth."

Zub said that his spaceship had broken down. He would be in trouble with his mum if he was late home for supper.

Longer sentences ✓

Wide range of vocabulary ✓

Varied and descriptive language ✓

Pictures provide opportunity for further discussion ✓